M. SOSKIN
December

ANDREW MARTIN

interior design review

volume 7

martin waller

dominic bradbury

belinda buckley

ANDREW MARTIN
INTERNATIONAL

Editor: Martin Waller

Text: Dominic Bradbury, Belinda Buckley

Project Executive: Annika Bowman

Product Design: Graphicom Design

First Published in 2003 by Andrew Martin International

ISBN 0-9530045-5-4

Reproduction by Yale Press. Printed in Great Britain by Butler and Tanner.

Acknowledgments

The authors and publisher wish to thank all the owners and designers of the projects
featured in this book.

They also thank the following photographers:

Ugur Atac, Fritz von der Schulenburg, Brian Benson, Winkelmann, Bertrand Limbour, Hans Fonk,
Henry Bourne, Caty Grunfeld, Winfried Heinze, Iain Kemp, Janne Peters, Bernd Boehm, Mona Gundersen,
James Hudson, 9H Imaging, Red Desert, Vania Toledo, Beto Riginik, Luke Foreman, Tim Goffe,
Andrew Florides, Christopher Cornwell, Reto Guntli, Marc Ninghetto, Giulio Oriani, Stefan Jannides,
Richard de Chaza, Richard Waite, Stephane Bravin, Tom Nitsch, Conor Horgan, Paul Sherwood,
Jean-Marie del Moral, Serdar Samli, Michael Calderwood, Jorge Pablo de Aguinaco, John Vaughn,
Douglas Keister, Andreas von Einsiedel, Gerald Steiner, Stephen Inngs, Warren Heath,
Pierre Yves Dhinaut, Marc Hertrich Property, David Liu @ IRP3, Michael Jäckel, Pom Lampson, Luis
Goncalves, Jose Miguel Figueiredo, Bruno Helbling Fotografie, Claudia Fagagnini of Fotodesign
Fagagnini, Doug McGregor, James Morris, Ales Jungmann, Ken Hayden, Barry Wallis, Tim Winter,
Dave Marlow, Michael Stepanov, Danie Nel, Niall Clutton, Ken Kirkwood, Solvi Dos Santos,
Andrew Wood, Hugo Burnand, John of John Gillan Photography, David Braun, Alain Proust,
Didier Delmas, Frederique Hornbostel, Chris Gascoigne, James Mortimer, Ray Main, Warren Smith,
John Renolds, Johnathan Cosh, Margaret M. de Lange, Joseph Sy.

introduction

What makes a great interior designer? The skills required are a quirky blend of the organisational and the artistic.

There are some essential attributes for any successful designer. Of course the sine qua non is a high level of accomplishment in the mechanics of the trade: the space planning, the marshalling of materials, the understanding of colour. But this counts for nothing if its not harnessed to a rigorous grasp of detail and a tenacious ability to get things done. Great schemes are soon forgotten if they are not implemented on time and in budget.

Perhaps what lifts a top designer above the crowd is their ability to bring something new to the arena. Its not enough to be a copier of previous work, however skilled. This is not as straightforward as it appears, because the designer's first priority is to realize the owners brief. Many clients are understandably nervous of designers indulging their fantasies, while their own aspirations are cast aside. That there is a perpetual tension here is amply demonstrated in this book's quotes. Some designers emphasise the primacy of the clients view and some underline the importance of the designers' own vision. Perhaps Kelly Hoppen expresses the balance best. 'Giving a client what they always wanted but didn't know they wanted until they had it.'

However the designer's greatest asset is personality. The best designers are all extraordinary characters, knowledgeable, erudite and witty. Designers irresistibly wield their ruthless charm in the eternal quest to make it happen. It's an education and a privilege to watch them in action.

Martin Waller

zeynep fadillioglu design

Designer: Zeynep Fadillioglu.
Company: Zeynep Fadillioglu
Design, Istanbul, Turkey.
Projects: Restaurants, clubs,
offices, shops, residential.

• Can't live without friends and family, cushion and a carpet, yoga and a phone • Luxury is a comfortable pair of shoes • Would ban injustice and politics triggered by religion • Gandhi is an icon • Mevlana Jalaluddin Rumi is a hero, Ed Tuttle is an influence, Sean Connery is the dinner date.

'All rules can be changed'

'I'm very serious about function, otherwise you just become a stylist'

rabih hage

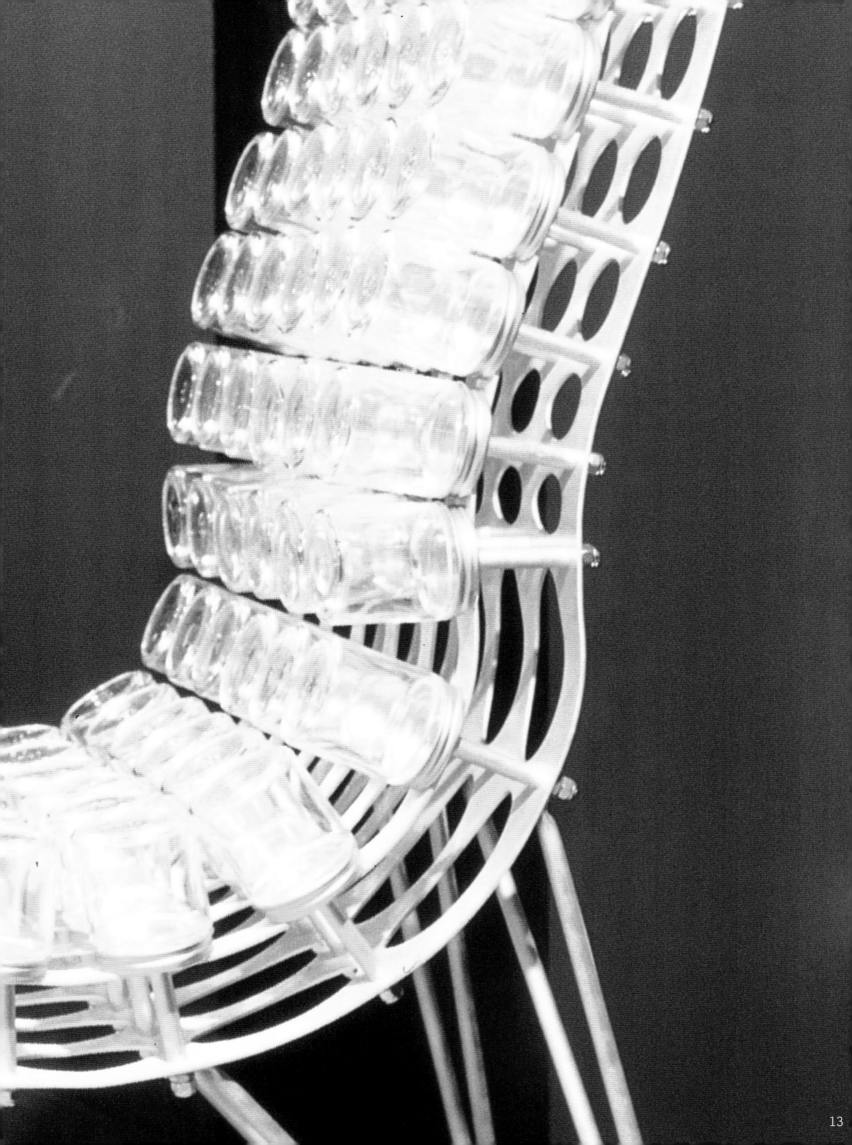

Designer: Rabih Hage. Company: Rabih Hage, London, UK. Projects: Mostly residential in Britain and France, some commercial work and furniture design.

- Would love to live in Eze in the South of France
- Frank Lloyd Wright is a hero, Paul Dupré-Lafon an influence, Claudia Schiffer a fantasy client • Hates zen and minimalism, likes Lagerfeld and Hendrix • Loves his work and his wife

'Putting spaces together is to do with emotions and emotions are personal'

'How the space will age is very important. I like interiors which defy time'

b.v.b.a

giardini

luigi giardini

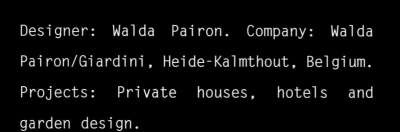

Designer: Walda Pairon. Company: Walda Pairon/Giardini, Heide-Kalmthout, Belgium. Projects: Private houses, hotels and garden design.

• Addicted to the rhythm of life • Afraid of losing time with worrying • Favourite luxuries are: drink champagne at her renaissance table, read Desert Flower by Waris Dirie, eat with Belgium's master chef Roger Souvereyns, stay at the Chateau de Bagnols in France.

'The Italian Renaissance is my favourite period and very influential for me, yet my work is essentially contemporary'

'I like wood,
linens, silk -
noble materials'

kit kemp

Designer: Kit Kemp. Company: Firmdale Hotels, London, UK. Projects: Hotels, restaurants and bars, plus occasional residential projects.

'If you are going to exaggerate it had better be good'

• Dreams of living in a gypsy caravan listening to the Doobie Brothers, reading Mary Webb • Addicted to paint colour charts and Vick's Vapour rub • Influenced by Vanessa Bell, Eileen Gray and David Mlinaric • Loves tea and toast first thing, hates painted lines on country roads.

'Interiors have to be meticulously
done to appear artless'

'I'm not one for playing around with different coloured lights and things; it gets gimmicky'

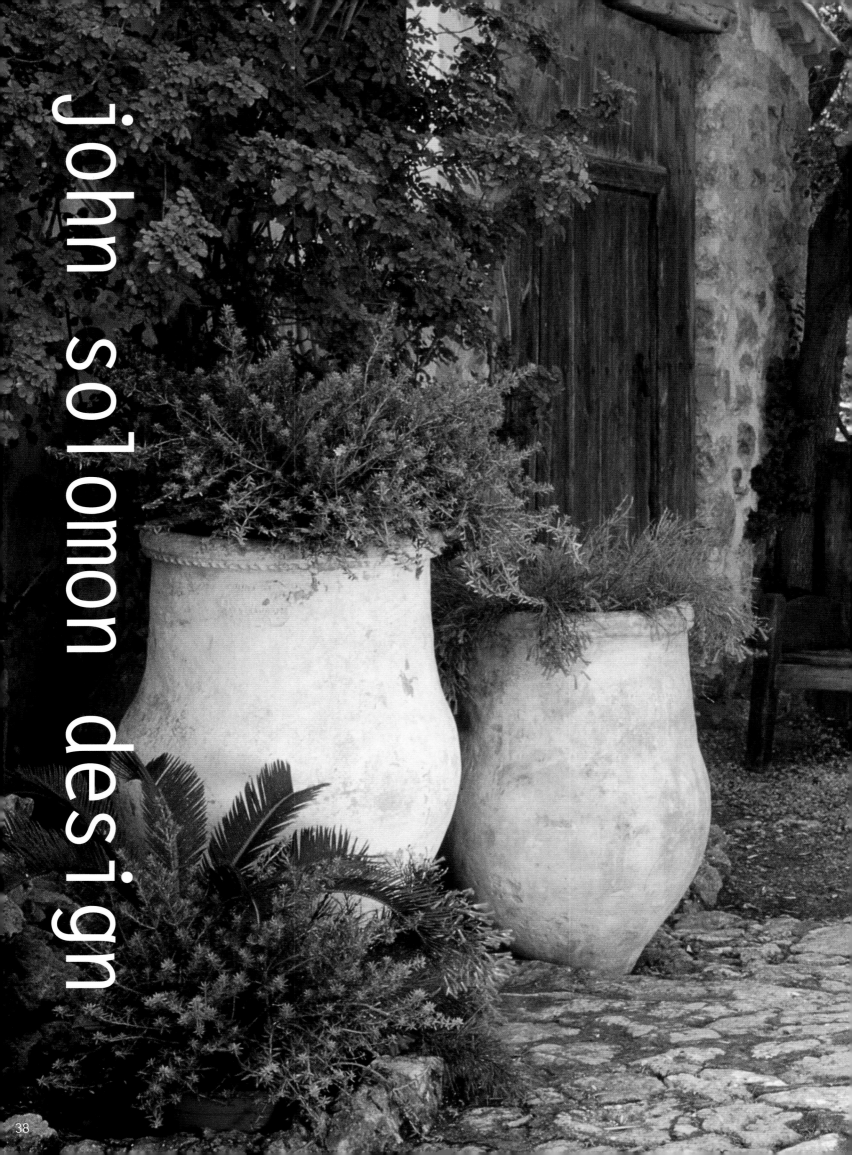

john solomon design

Designer: John Solomon. Company: John Solomon Design, Richmond, UK. Projects: London townhouses and private properties from rural to royal.

- Greatest luxury is his holiday home by the sea
- Would ban chewing gum and fluorescent lighting
- Influenced by Shaw, wears Sander, listens to Schubert
- Addicted to gadgets, can't live without a garden.

'My design rules consist simply of proportion, proportion, proportion'

taylor howes designs

Designers: Gail Taylor and Karen Howes. Company: Taylor Howes Designs, London, UK. Projects: Primarily residential, including show apartments, as well as health spas, hotels and offices.

Covet a home with lots of glass, overlooking the ocean • Dalai Lama is their hero • Audrey Hepburn is the epitome of style • Armani and Valentino are favourite tailors, Ralph Lauren and Donna Karan are major influences • Carpe diem is best advice, breakfast in bed best ambition.

'Create for your client's requirements and don't live out your own fantasy'

51

'Lose the clutter and you will feel a much better person for it'

jane ainscough design

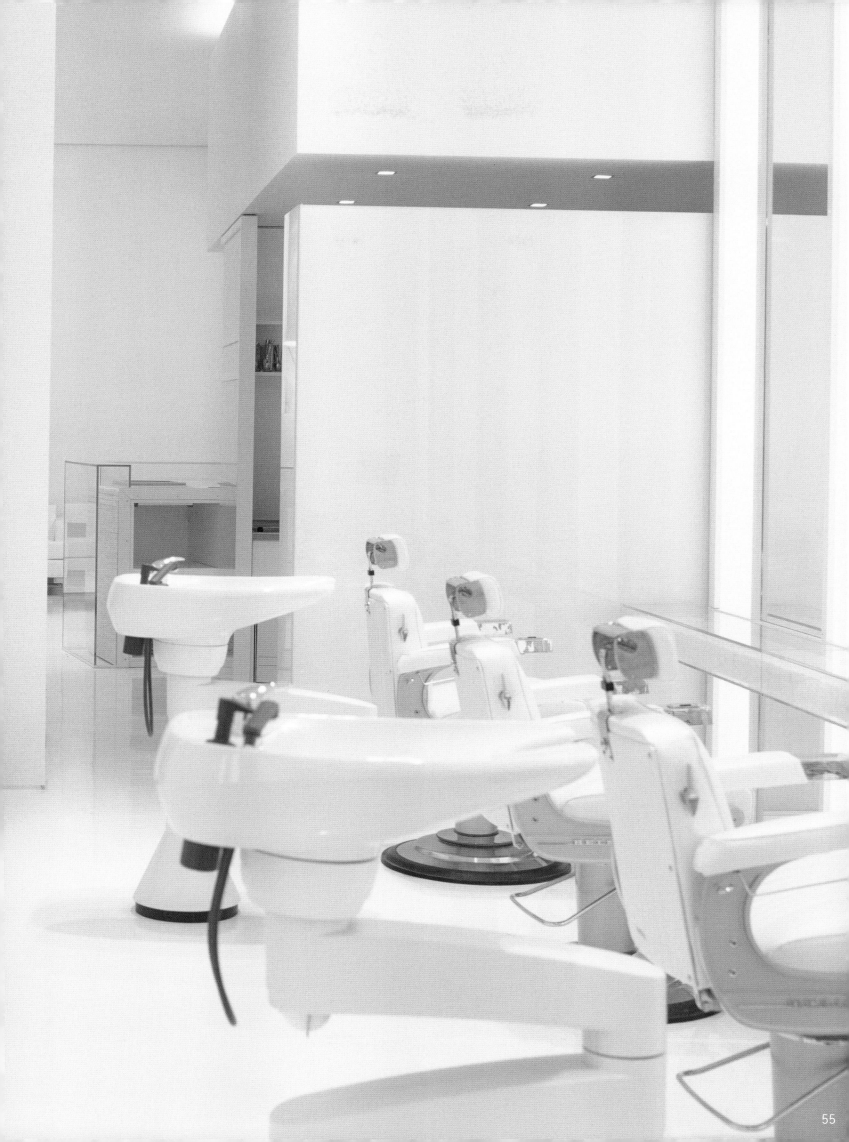

Designer: Jane Ainscough. Company: Jane Ainscough Design, Hamburg, Germany. Projects: Residential and commercial, especially store design.

● The perfect home would be a run down villa on Lake Maggiore to renovate room by room ● Rem Koolhaas and Louise Borgeois are heroes ● Admires Miuccia Prada, fancies Hugh Grant, rates Ben Bradlee, proudest of two daughters ● Must have handbags, fresh flowers, sunglasses, salt and vinegar crisps.

'If you look at a building like a body, there are certain attributes that should be enhanced and others that should be disguised

'I love minimalism and modernism'

'It's good to take a notebook because inspiration is everywhere - nature, film, music'

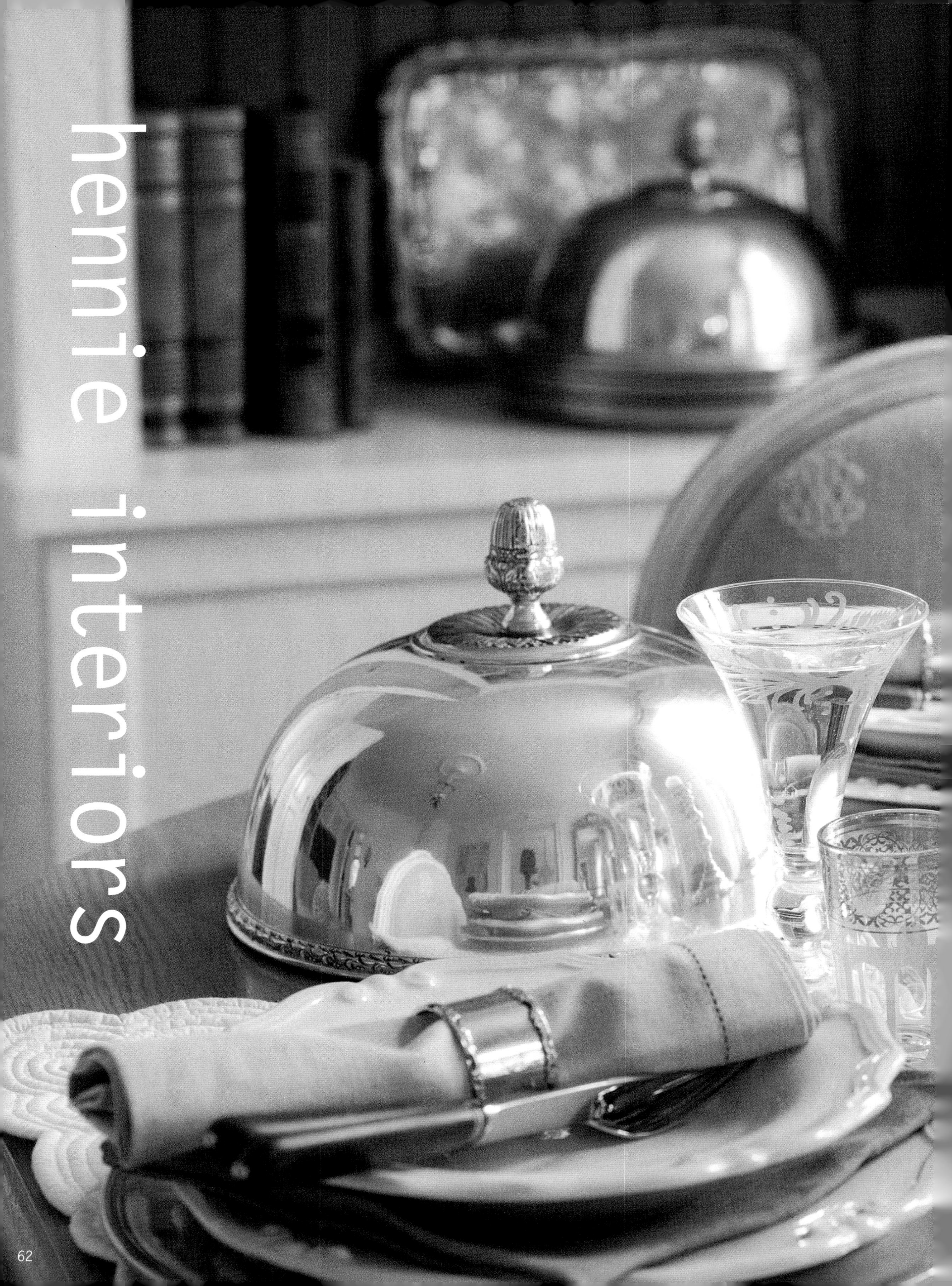

hennie interiors

Designer: Helene Hennie.
Company: Hennie Interiors,
Oslo, Norway. Projects:
Residential, mainly in
Norway.

• Can't live without people she loves and Pomerol '75 • Family is the ultimate luxury • Loves Leonardo da Vinci, Armani and the Villa d' Este • Would ban the 1980s • Constantly developing teamwork and creativity are the keys to success.

'The setting of a house is very significant. We are working on a lot of cabins in the mountains where you are part of nature and you are always looking out as well as in'

'There will always be a little

bit of Scandinavia in what we do'

cream

Designer: Tony Chan. Company: Cream, Hong Kong. Projects: Warehouse apartments and town houses.
• Would like to live in an ulta modern home in 16th century France with Chairman Mao, Madonna and Cleopatra for dinner •
Favourite movies: Ben Hur and Bladerunner
• Terrified of losing the data on his computer • True luxury is sleep.

'Lighting is a source of energy as well as illumination'

joão mansur

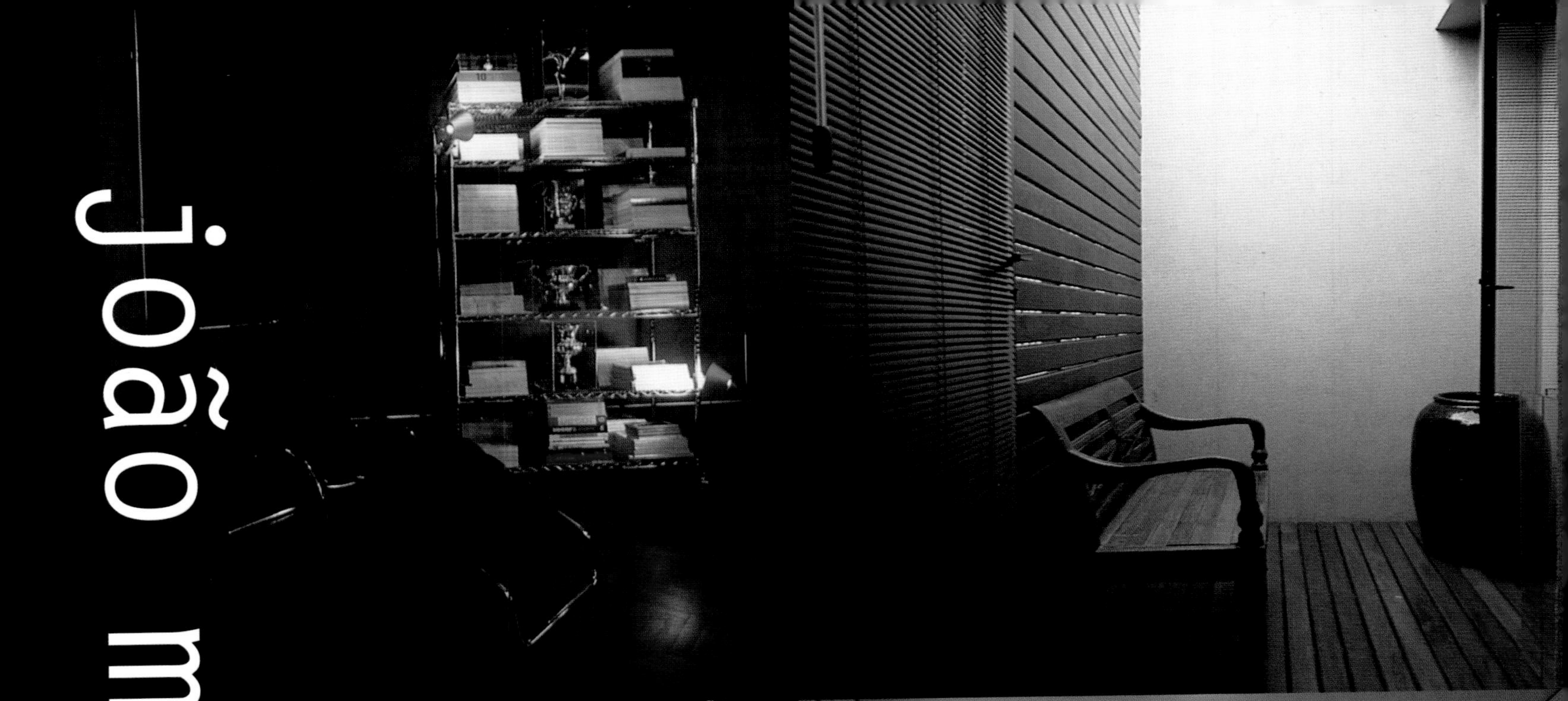

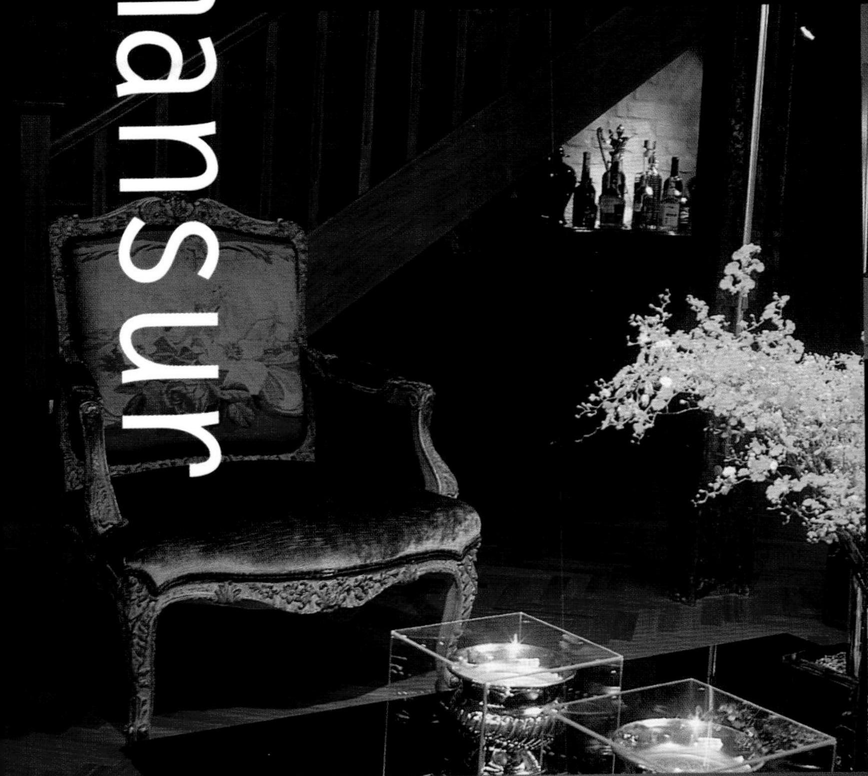

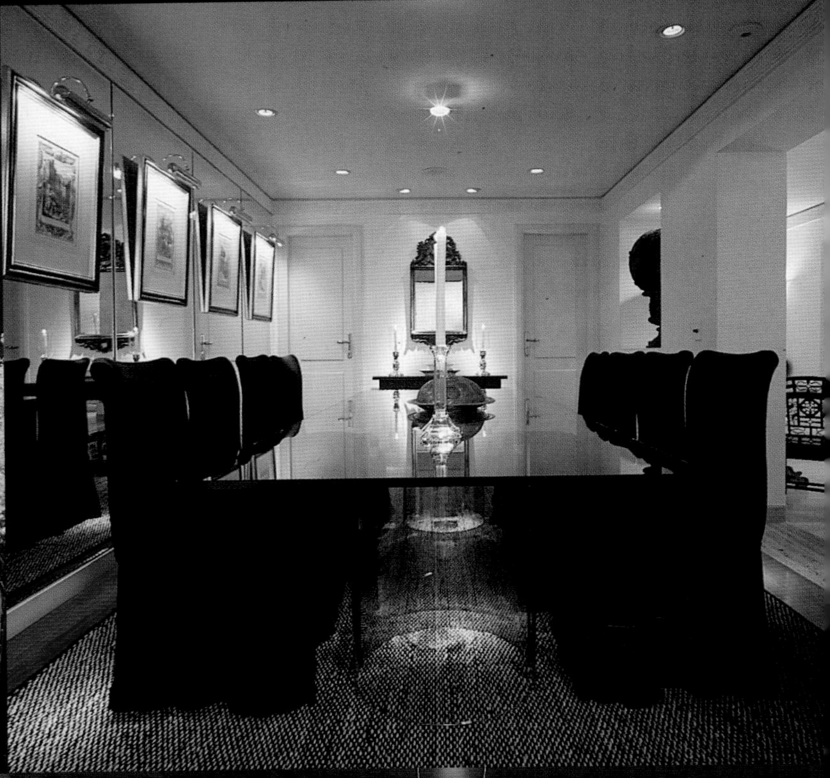

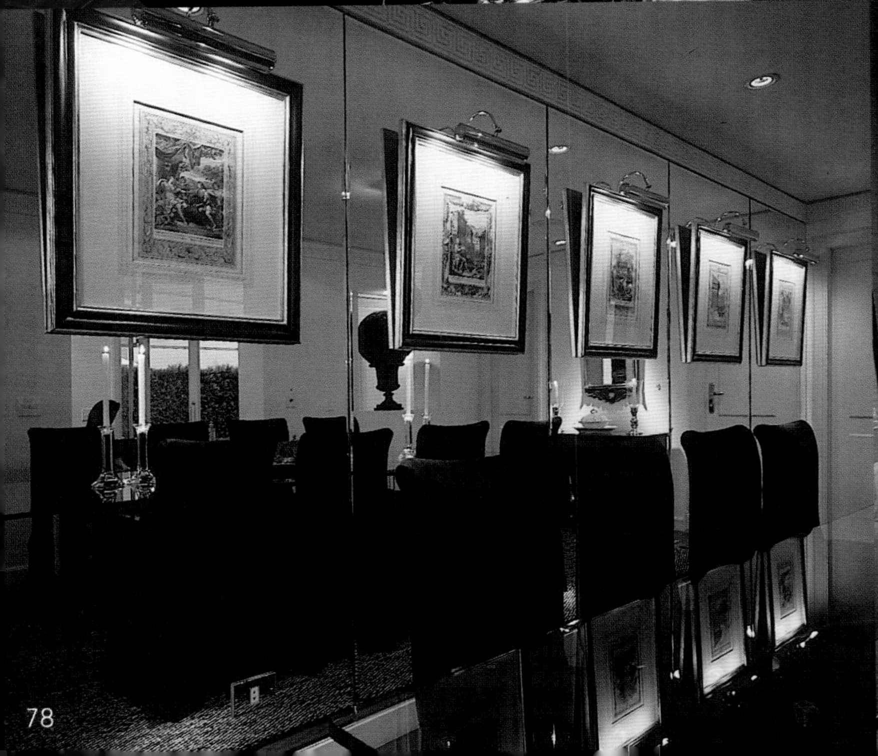

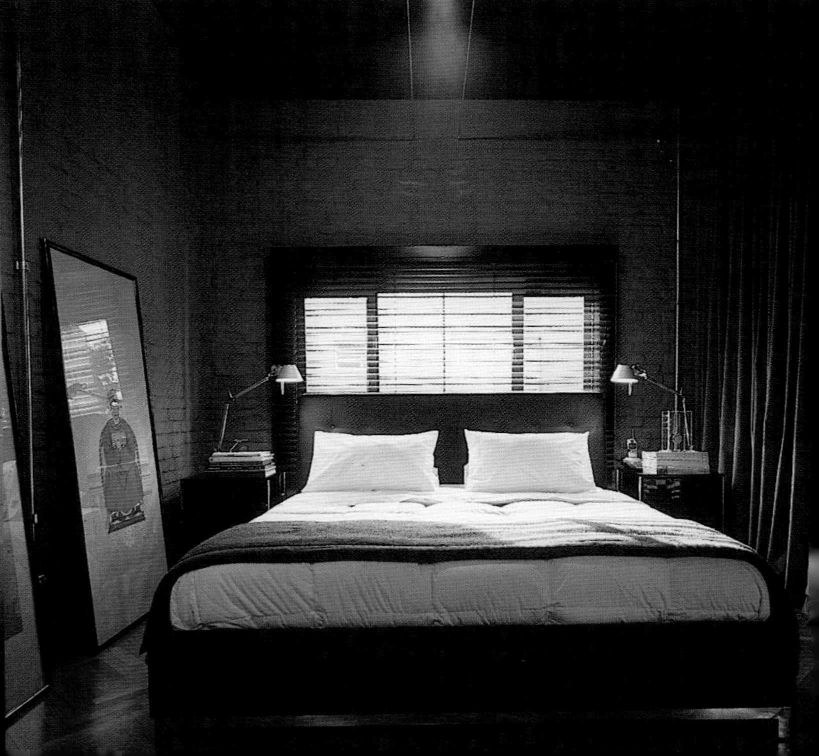

Designer: João Mansur. Company: João Mansur Architecture & Design, Sao Paulo, Brazil. Projects: Restaurants, shops and homes.

• Aspires to a Haussmannian apartment in Parc Monceau in Paris • Can't live without comfort and quality • Jackie Kennedy and Napoleon are icons, Grace Kelly the perfect dinner date, the Plaza Athenée in Paris the perfect hotel.

• Loves breakfast, shopping, working • Hates bad taste.

'Flexibility is the key to a new way of living'

'You should never get lost in fashion and trends'

tara bernerd

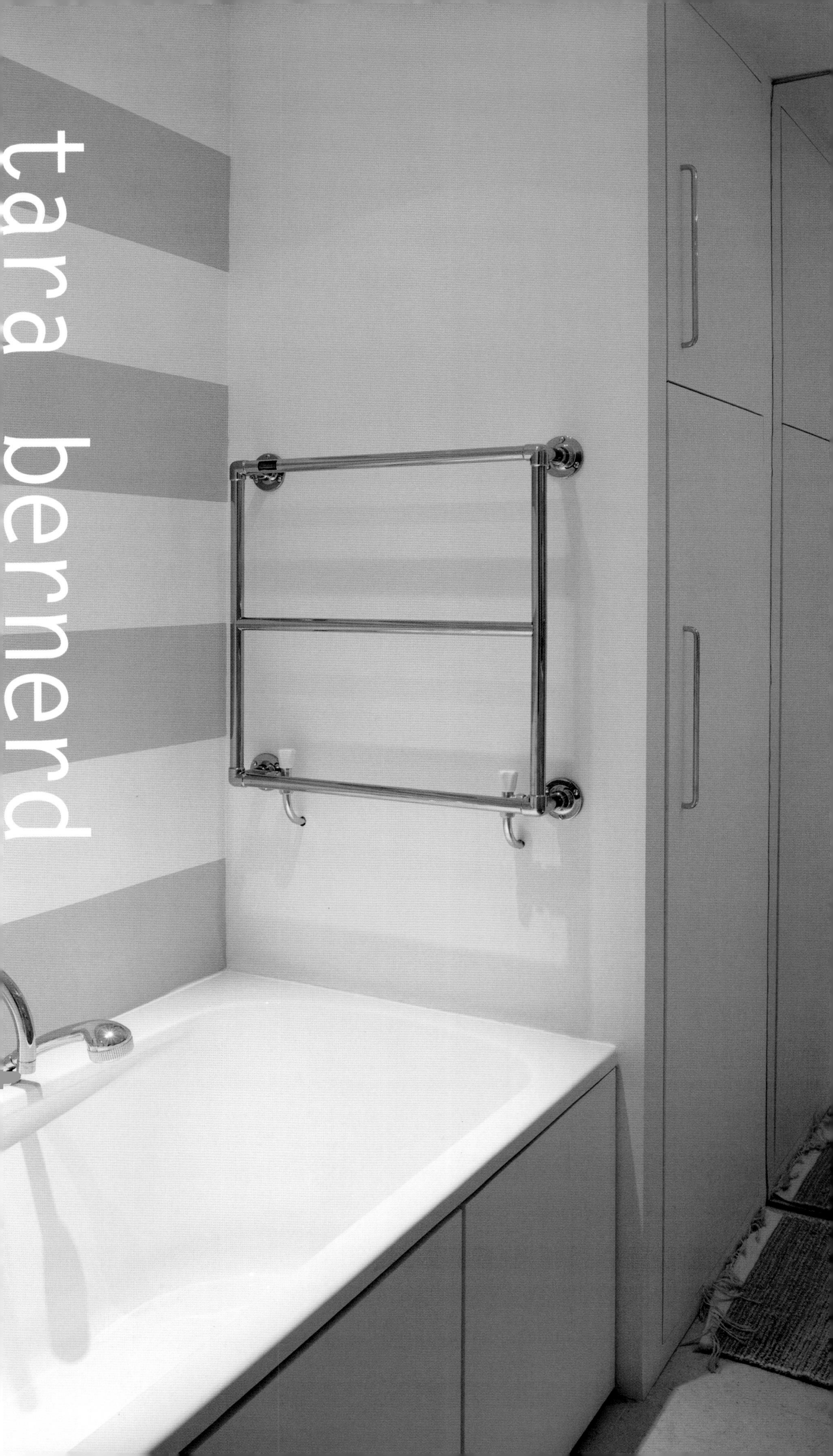

'I'm using leather, velvet, satin'

Designer: Tara Bernerd. Company: Target Living. Projects: Architecture, interiors and furniture design. Mainly houses and apartments, including residential development projects, and commercial work such as art galleries.

• Addicted to colour (except peach) and always had a thing for leather club chairs and Jim Morrison • Paul Smith has impeccable taste and great vision and Luis Barragan tremendous style • Afraid of fear, dreads the gym loves Vivienne Westwood • Martha Stewart is an influence, John Malkovich a fantasy.

'It's important to step back and not be too clever'

Designer: Terrie Wixon Gibbs. Company: Wixon Gibbs, Hampton, UK. Projects: Private houses and apartments, plus shops and some commercial work.

• Dreams of building her own home • Couldn't live without her reference books • Brunel, Lutyens, Calder and Jellicoe are icons • Eddie Izzard is the ideal date • Frightened of

snakes • Loves Radio 4 •
Addicted to tea, coffee
and life.

'Minimalism has been a fantastic
learning curve but it's not individual
and I love things to be individual'

isherwood design

Designer: Pip Isherwood. Company: Isherwood Interior Design, Cheltenham, UK. Projects: Mostly residential, some commercial, and nationwide across the UK.

• Dream home would be a glass box with amazing sea views and lots of domestic staff • Can't live without art, white tops and jeans • Mark Rothko and Nelson Mandela are icons, but dinner with the cast of Oceans Eleven is good • Having cream tea dressed in a hotel's (Hotel Splendido in Portofino) white fluffy robe is the great luxury • Tom and Olli are the proudest moments.

'Colour precision is important to us. We will use the same colour in adjacent finishes and spend a lot of time matching them exactly'

christopher chang

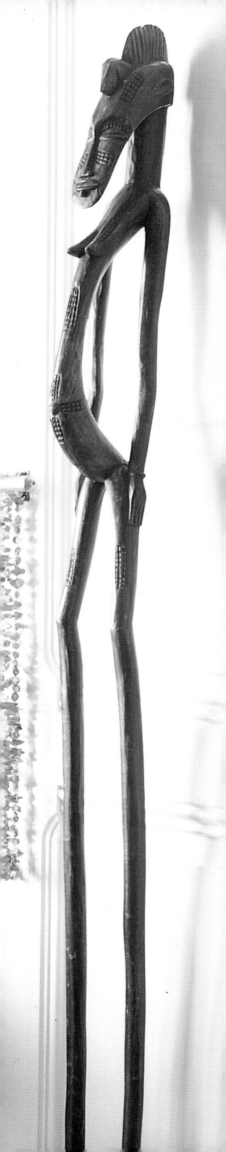

Designers: Christophe
Interior Design, Ge
Switzerland, Britain

'The work is complex in its simplicity'

colour can have a powerful effect on one's mood

• Covets an abandoned house in the countryside to restore to splendour • First performance dancing at the Geneva Opera House is the proudest moment but addicted to interior design • Influenced by John Saladino and Albert Hadley • Admires Manolo Blahnik's detailing, Andrea Palladio and Jean-Michel Frank are icons • Likes to stay at La Maison Arabe in Marrakesh and read V.S. Naipaul.

'We love diversity'

'We don't believe there's any
one recipe to suit all clients'

claudia pelizzari

Designer: Claudia Pelizarri.
Company: Claudia Pelizarri
Interior Design, Brescia,
Lombardy, Italy. Projects:
Mainly residential villas in
northern Italy.

• Hero worships Virginia Woolf, and Philippe Starck • Influenced by Axel Vervoort • Wears Comme des Garçons, reads English drama, fearful of an increasingly violent world • Addicted to shopping in London • Can't live without the countryside, hates wasting water.

'The idea is to maintain the unique historic atmosphere of the house, while implementing non-intrusive modern techniques'

'The style of my work is intimate and essential'

'Opt for colours and clear

'lighting inspired by nature'

monica blinco

interior design

'I implement quite a Southern European look on to our hot Australian canvas'

Designer: Monica Blinco. Company: Monica Blinco Interior
Design, Hamilton, Queensland, Australia. Projects: High
profile residential.

• Meditates every morning • Loves the Four Seasons in Bali • Would like dinner
with Jeremy Irons • Best read is Coco & Igor by Chris Greenhalgh • Best clothes
by Valentino and Yves Saint Laurent • Hero worships Ralph Lauren and her mother.

'I'm really into using satin fabrics

lifestyles

Designer: Joanna Burston. Company: Lifestyles Interiors, London, UK.
Projects: Mostly residential, including houses, apartments and show homes.

'In our last project we had a talking wall that you spoke to, with all the technology hidden away. You told it what CD you wanted, told it when you were leaving the house so it could turn on the security'

• Wants a beach house somewhere very hot • Addicted to sunshine and handbags • Fantasy dinner date is her husband • Couldn't live without her dog • Admires John Saladino, Armani, Architectural Digest and Chicago • Would outlaw coloured bathroom suites.

'My golden rule is always overscale'

Aroma in a home is very important, cedar wood in the study, fresh floral in a bedroom. People underestimate how the scent of a room can be as 'important as the way it looks'

Designer: Andrew Winch. Company: Andrew Winch Designs, London, UK. Projects: Predominantly custom leisure and sail yachts, but also planes and houses.

• Dream home would be a house by the sea with a small sail boat • Can't live without water to look at and time to sail • Loves Van Morrison, James Bond and staying at the Chateau de la Chevre d'Or on the Cote d'Azur • Afraid of failure • Addicted to design • Inspired by Jon Bannenberg.

'Our clients have a dream'

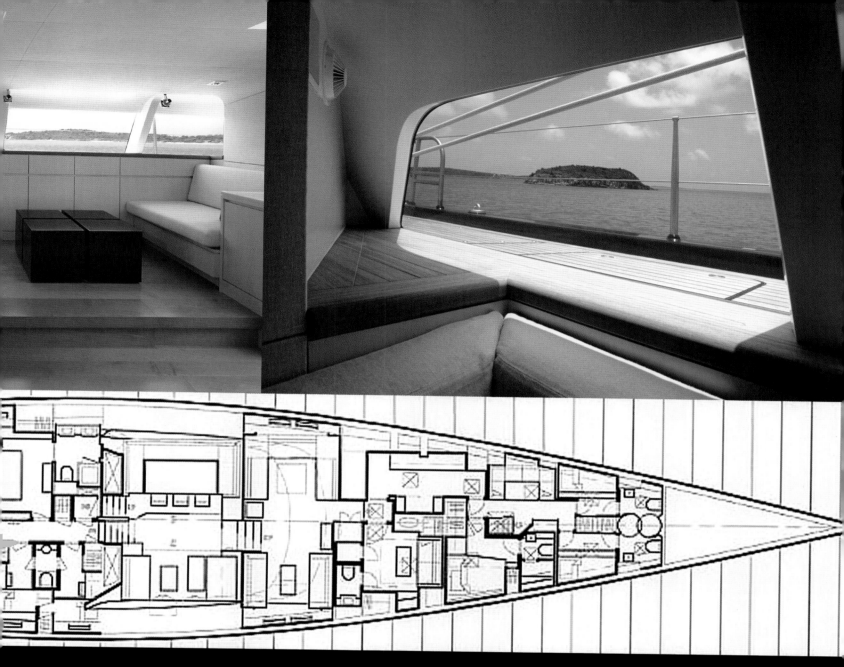

'Simplify, listen to the client and launch the boat'

merrion square interiors

Designers: Helen Roden and Joe Ensko. Company: Merrion Square Interiors, Dublin, Ireland. Projects: Warehouse apartments in central Dublin.

• Listen to Albinoni • Read vintage books on interiors • Wear Tom Ford and Prada • Like Claridges and All About Eve • Addicted to travel, cashmere and champagne.

'We love scouring markets and auction houses for inspirational pieces'

'We often use strong colours to accent and lift a neutral backdrop'

Designer: Broosk Saib. Company: Broosk Saib, London, UK. Projects: Residential, mostly in Britain plus some work internationally.

- Japanese food is an indulgence, holidays a preference, hot water an essential • Zaha Hadid, Robert Adam, Ralph Lauren are inspirations • Enjoys political comment, hates politicians • Would like to watch Hitchcock, listen to Dvorak, dine with Oscar Wilde.

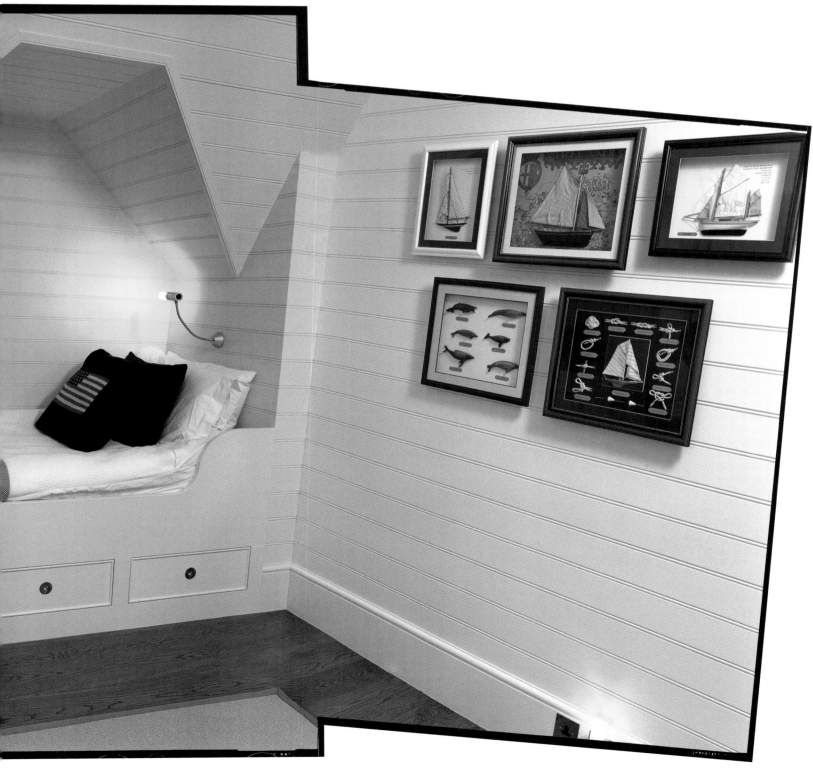

'When people say they are so relaxed in a home that's the greatest compliment anyone can give'

serdar gül gün

Designer: Serdar Gülgün. Company: Serdar Gülgün, Istanbul, Turkey. Projects: Residential interior design, exhibition design, fabric, furniture and porcelain design.

• Can't live without comfort • Would love dinner with Madame de Pompadour or any royal mistress • Would ban cheap theatricality in houses and personality • Favourites are Marilyn Monroe and glamour, Yves Saint Laurent and Tangier, Ella Fitzgerald and cooking.

'My work is Ottoman revisited'

jacobs

design

Designer: Jerry Jacobs.
Company: Jacobs Design, Northern California, USA.
Projects: Villas in Cancun and the Mexican Caribbean, modern town houses in Mexico City.

• Addicted to fresh air, good food and beautiful views • Most influenced by Norman Foster • Best film is Sexy Beast, best fashion Ermenegildo Zegna, best hotel Villa Santa Monica in Mexico • Would ban weapons and mediocre design.

'I'm keen on playing with mirrors to reflect views and distort reality'

casa nova

Designer: Wessel von Loringhoven. Company: Casa Nova, Dusseldorf, Germany. Projects: Mainly residential.

• A turn of the century house above San Francisco Bay with a substantial garage is ideal • Historic sports cars are his indulgence, racing them his passion • Loves Ella, Cole Porter, Coco Chanel, the Hotel San Vigilio on Lake Garda and his wife • Frightened of clients with Persian rugs.

architecture

vie interieur
et décoration d'intérieur

'We love working with zinc, leather, reclaimed timber, gravel and unusual natural textiles'

Designers: Philip Pelletier and Francesco Saporita. Company: Vie Interieur, Neuchatel, Switzerland. Projects: directional restaurants and contemporary residential.

• Can't live without love, sunshine, lust for life • Rate Leonardo and Michaelangelo, Lionel Richie and Louis Armstrong, Asterix and Obelix • Would ban excessive ambition and navel gazing.

irma mcpherson

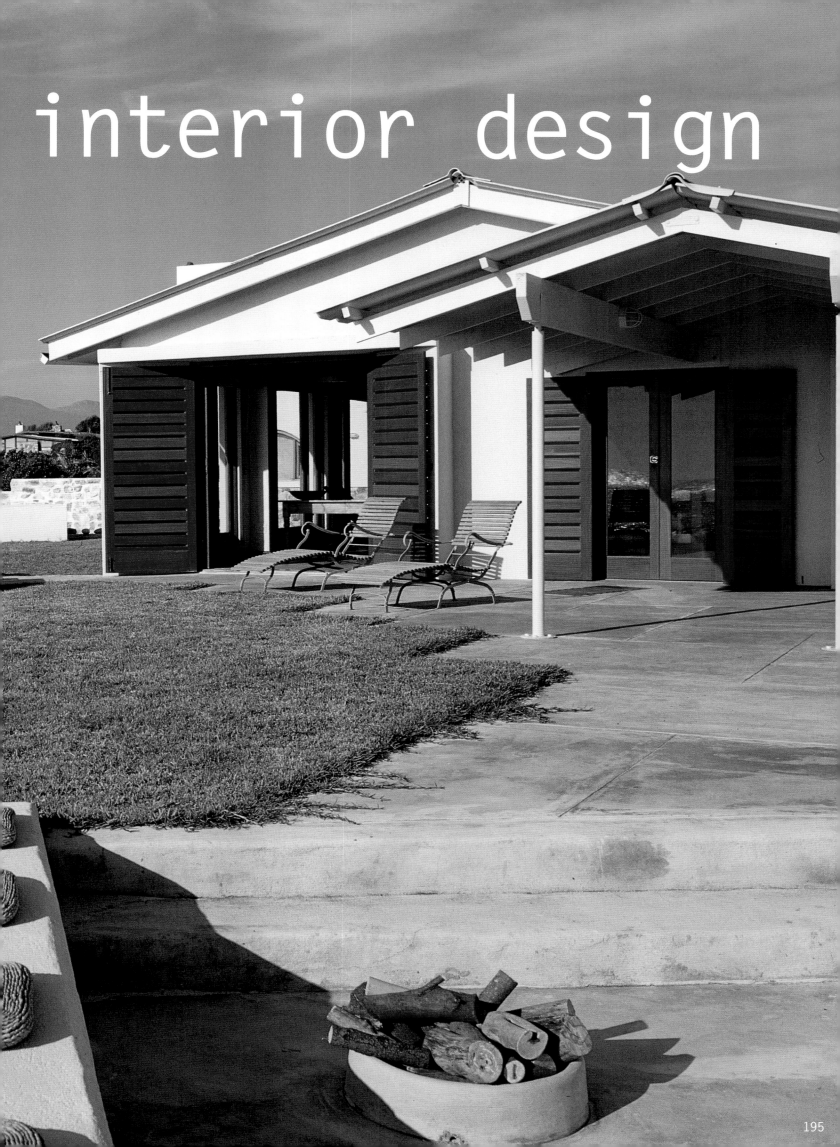

interior design

'An interior should hold surprises'

Designer: Irma McPherson. Company: Irma McPherson Interior Design, Cape Town, South Africa. Projects: Mainly residential, in South Africa.

• The ideal home would be a converted barn in Normandy, filled with books and Rudolf Nureyev and Margot Fonteyn as guests • Frédéric Méchiche is the biggest influence, the Oriental Bangkok the best place to stay and the Cape Times the essential morning read • Likes ice cream, hates snakes, admires Carolyn Quartermaine.

marc hertrich

Designers: Marc Hertrich and Nicolas Adnet. Company: Marc Hertrich & Co, Paris, France. Projects: Hotels, restaurants, bars and residential projects in France, Portugal and Switzerland.

● Can't live without books, paper and pens ● Addicted to discovering other cultures, countries, ideas and ways of life ● Wants time to do other things ● Listens to Philip Glass, enjoys Pedro

Almodóvar's films, reads biographies, wears Paul Smith • Jesus and Louis XIV are heroes.

'Within the design of a restaurant we try to let diners choose different atmospheres in the same space'

205

接 待
RECEPTION

chhada siembieda

& associates

Designers: Chandu Chhada and Henry Leung. Company: Chhada Siembieda & Associates Limited, Hong Kong. Projects: Five star hotels in India, China and South East Asia.

• Loves Armani, Fiddler on the Roof and Indian Nobel Prize winner Rabindranath Tagor • On rising prays and meditates each morning • Would ban violence and dreams of living in permanent peace and prosperity • Influenced by Le Corbusier and Frank Lloyd Wright but his parents are his heroes.

'Requirements of
a guest room are
clean   air,   a
comfortable bed,
immaculate bath-
room, good desk
and   a   perfect
bedside   reading
light'

azul-tierra

Designer: Antonio Espuch. Company: Azul-Tierra, Alicante, Spain. Projects: Residential and commercial, including restaurants and offices.

• Addicted to work • To do what you want is the greatest indulgence • Can't live with pretentious things or without a warm atmosphere • Favourite hotel is always a friends house • Heroes are Begona Zunzunegui and Roberto Mira.

'I like any natural materials'

interiors bis

'We always try to follow clean design lines for an uncluttered look'

Designers: James Moore, Arabella Allsopp and Andrea Sedgwick. Company: Interiors Bis, London, UK. Projects: Mainly residential refurbishments in London.

• Love the Hotel Bel-Ami in Paris, top quality stationery and watching Roman Holiday • Addicted to sushi from Itsu and Sainsbury's Sancerre • Believe in always questioning authority • Would love dinner with David Hicks and Ann Boyd

- Would ban small mean cushions, valances on sofas and yellow teeth.

'Show off the beauty of the main materials.'

'don't make too much of the extraneous'

manuel francisco

jorge interiores

Designer: Manuel Francisco Jorge. Company: MFJ Interiores, Lisbon, Portugal. Projects: Mainly private homes.

• Mies van der Rohe is a hero, David Hicks an influence, Tom Ford a favourite • Bad taste should be banned, less is more should be law • Afraid of dying, addicted to love, bereft without a mirror.

'I rely on historical references - especially Art Deco and the 1940s'

sue rohrer

Designer: Sue Rohrer. Company: Sue Rohrer Zumikon, Zumikon, Switzerland. Projects: Mainly residential, some commercial.

● A big old barn in the mountains near St Moritz would be the dream home ● Can't live without harmony in partnerships, friendships and home ● Likes Rod Stewart and Jung Chang ● Admires Nelson Mandela and Martin Luther King ● Influenced by Anouska Hempel and Frédéric Méchiche ● Wears Dolce & Gabbana.

artus inneneinrichtung

239

Designer: Markus Beat Stoll. Company: Artus, Zug, Switzerland. Projects: Large residences throughout Europe.

• Influenced by Jean Michel Frank • Loves Italian palazzos and Princess Diana • Addicted to good living, good food and good wine • Reads Wallpaper, admires Etro, listens to Sinatra • Likes staying in the Kempinski Hotel Adlon in Berlin.

'I like to introduce subtle drama to a limited palette by altering paint finishes, either matt or gloss'

jestico and whiles

Designers: Sniez Torbarina, with James Dilley, Angus Eitel, Michelle Le Masurier, Francois Bertrand, Christine Correard, Sureeporn Chuatirarak, Geraldine Knight and director Jophn Whiles. Company: Jestico & Whiles, London, UK. Projects: Hotels, restaurants, bars, museums, stations and residential.

• Wants a glass house on a Dalmatian island • Most influenced by Le Corbusier and Eileen Gray • Would ban bad manners and make smiling universal • Time is the great luxury and Coco Chanel a heroine • Reading biographies and grabbing an extra moment of sleep are special pleasures.

'We are aiming to create modern classics, with a philosophy that mixes twentieth century modernism with the language of the 21st century'

sriberg associates

Designer: Susan Sriberg. Company: Sriberg Associates, London, UK. Projects: High end residential in London and the USA, as well as period restorations.

• Wants to live in a glass pavilion in a Capability Brown landscape • Icons are Jimmy Carter and Andree Putman • Listens to Bach, wears Karl Lagerfeld • Scared of the dentist • Addicted to coffee.

'I like to think that I create homes,
rather than decorating houses'

michael attenborough

Designer: Michael Attenborough. Company: Radisson Edwardian Hotels, UK. Projects: New builds and refurbishments for hotels.

• Dreams of living in an Ibizan villa • Long lunches with friends are the greatest indulgence • Favourite movies: Cat on a Hot Tin Roof, Moulin Rouge • Would ban prejudice and junk mail • Addicted to fun • Frightened of failure.

'Durability and practicality with timeless elegance, does mean spending that bit more - it always pays off in the end'

associates III

Designers: Kari Foster, Annette Stelmack, Maggie Tandysh, Donna Barta-Winfield, Beth Scott, Angie Pache. Company: Associates III, Denver, Colorado, USA.

• None can live without family, water, a measuring tape and scales • Spoil themselves with vacations and spa treatments • Fearful of further depleting the Earth's natural resources • Tragically addicted to work and chocolate.

'Organization, attention to detail and quick response are the keys to success'

artistic design

Designer: Dmitry Velikovsky. Company:
Artistic Design, Moscow, Russia.
Projects: Penthouses in Moscow.

• Greatest luxury is free time but can't live without regular trips to Asia • Most influenced by John Saladino, most bothered by the thought of losing interest • Likes reading memoirs but not romantic enough to have heroes • Wouldn't ban anything even bad taste: its diversity that makes things interesting.

'People should get rid of the things they have no affection for'

'Its great to give people much more than they expect from a scheme'

'I call my style eclectic minimalism'

dq&w design

Designers: Du Quesne du Plessis and Werner van Blerk. Company: D Q & W Design, Cape Town, South Africa. Projects: Offices of a top model agency as well as residences around Cape Town.

• Can't live without pristine white sheets and exercise • Influenced by Liagre and Mies Van der Rohe • Icons: Mandela, Picasso and Dali • Favourites: Bertolucci, Thierry Mugler, Gabriel Garcia Marquez • Hates: fake plants, fluorescent lighting • Addictions: romance, massage and chocolate.

'If you allow your client's personality to shine through your work, then you are going to create something of lasting value and the project won't date for your customer'

hunt hamilton zuch

ALGUES

Designer: Lynne Hunt. Company: Hunt Hamilton Zuch Ltd, London, UK. Projects: Carlton Tower Hotel, Knightsbridge, London and Hyde Park Gate serviced appartments.

• Influenced by Emile-Jacques Ruhlmann and Sir Terence Conran • Likes staying at Claridges and La Reserve on the French Riviera • Religiously reads The Daily Telegraph every Saturday • Wouldn't ban anything but would make it obligatory to be kind • Indulges herself with chips, addicted to Diet Coke, frightened of spiders, loves her children.

'A paint's finish can create so much

'more interest than its colour alone'

constanze

interior projects

Designer: Constanze von Unruh.
Company: Constanze Interior
Projects, Richmond, UK.
Projects: Anything from a
beach residence to commercial
fit outs.

• Icons are Coco Chanel and Philippe Starck • Would like Steve McQueen as dinner date • Listens to Miles Davies, watches Pulp Fiction, wears Jil Sander • Hates Mexican food and badly designed hospitals.

'As my background is in psychology, I am very interested in the human experience within all forms of space. In any context, either formal or relaxed, I try to create environments for wellbeing. Christopher Alexander's book 'A Pattern Language' has brought about a major shift in my thinking of how to arrange space'

'Contemporary and minimal stand increasingly for blandness'

'Design is a continuous learning process and one should never stop educating the eye through art, travel, books, film, theatre and society'

b. pila design studio

Designer: Beatrice Pila Gonzalez. Company: B. Pila Design Studio, Miami, Florida, USA. Projects: Mainly residential in and around Miami.

• Values stunning views, good food and magazines • Influenced by Robert Stern and Michael Graves, wears Diane von Furstenburg and Anne Klein • Frightened of not getting enough done • Allows herself just one cup of coffee in the morning • Would ban hate • Can't exist without faith.

'Usually a building's architecture has something to say and I always listen to that'

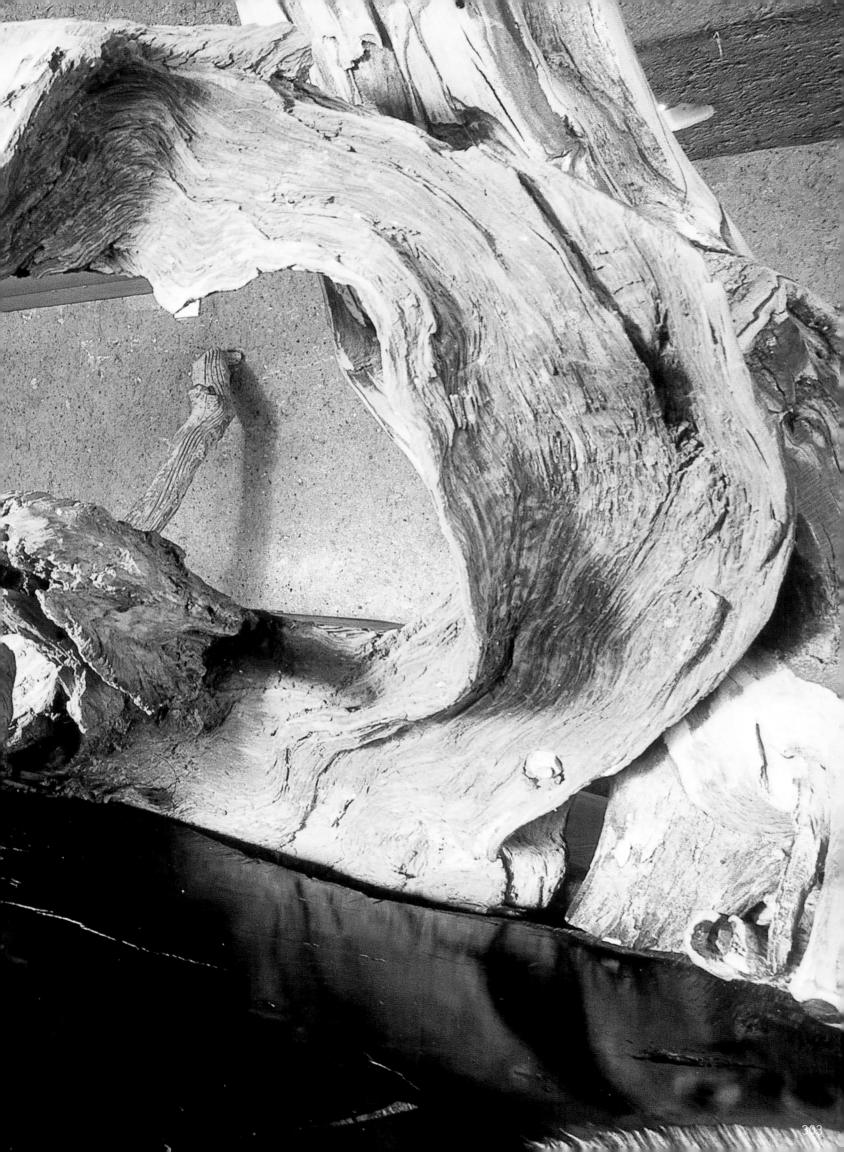

Designer: Jacqui Loon.
Company: Sabi Sabi Private
Game Reserve, South Africa.
Project: Earth Lodge, near
Shukuza, deep in the bushveld.

• Heroes are Nelson Mandela and Lucien Freud • Would have liked dinner with Mahatma Ghandi • Can't live without beauty and order, frightened of losing faculties and dignity in old age • Dreams of living atop a mountain overlooking the sea.

'Bespoke furniture is inspired by animal and plant shapes, with stool legs like rhino horns and sculputure carved from old local trees'

kelly hopper

interiors

Designer: Kelly Hoppen. Company: Kelly Hoppen Interiors, London, UK. Projects: High end residential 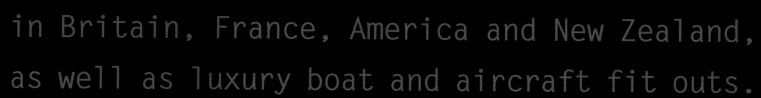 in Britain, France, America and New Zealand, as well as luxury boat and aircraft fit outs.

• Dreams of living by the sea and dinner with Robert Redford • Icon is Marilyn Monroe • Favourite movie Sound of Music • Likes La Scalinatella on Capri • Would ban drugs and war • Wears Alexander McQueen, Prada and Amanda Wakely.

'My trademark is very individual now, sort of a couture approach to decorating, as I'm very adept at giving a client what they always wanted, but didn't know they wanted until they had it. Once I crack that the rest just follows'

'I would say that I am a purist rather than a minimalist'

s.b.interiors

Designers: Sandra Billington and Guillermo Estenoz. Company: S.B. Interiors, Marbella, Spain. Projects: Houses and apartments, including show apartments, mostly in Spain.

• Addicted to antiques, afraid of budgets • Loves Breakfast at Tiffany's, Armani and Architectural Digest • Would ban over bright lighting • Gaudi is the ideal dinner guest, The Berkeley the place to stay.

'When you have so much sun and colour outside, it's good to work with a neutral palette'

thorp design

Designer: Philippa Thorp. Company: Thorp Design, London, UK. Projects: KXGym and private residences.

- Loves Valentino, Breakfast at Tiffany's and Aman Puri
- Hates heights, likes diamonds • Would ban road noise and DIY programmes
- Favourite tune Simply the Best by Tina Turner
- Insists on bedside reading lights.

about making sure that the client enjoys

the whole process; service is everything'

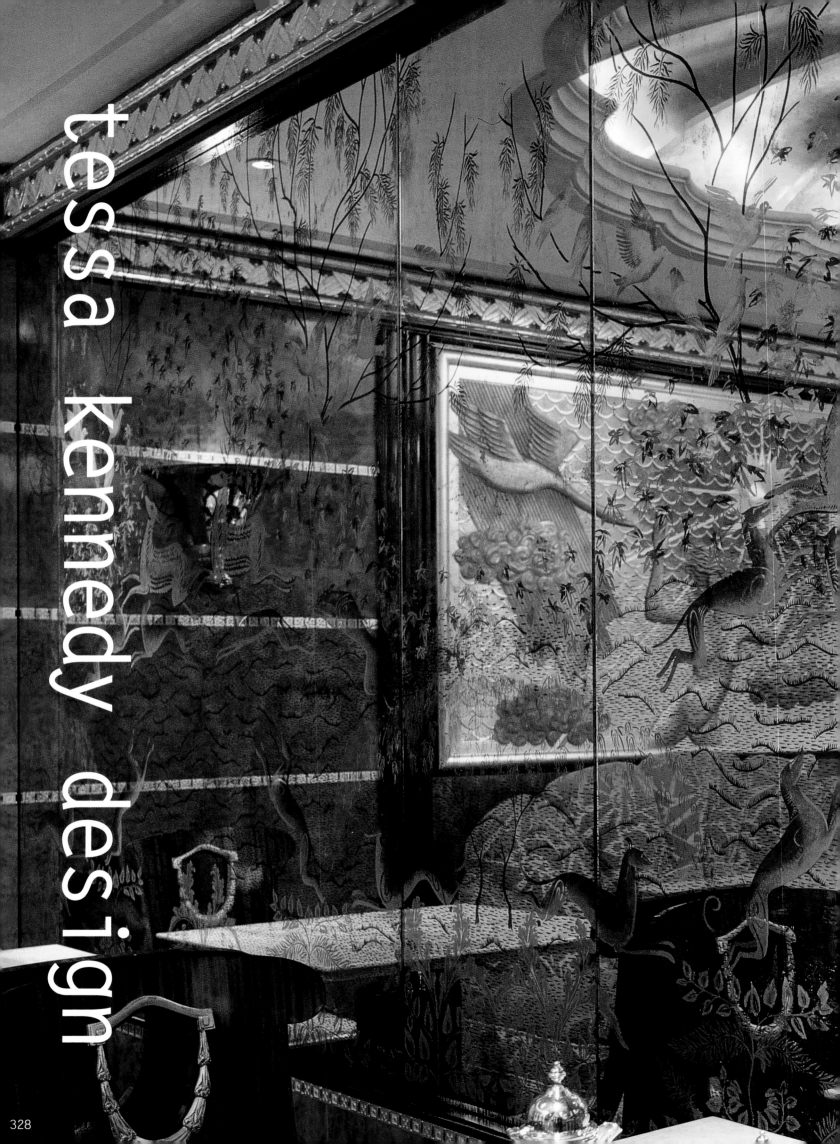

tessa kennedy design

'I always follow the classical order of architecture - I find it fatal to go against it'

THE TIVOLI BAR
AT THE RITZ

330

Designer: Tessa Kennedy. Company: Tessa Kennedy Design, London, UK. Projects: 5 star hotels, high end residential and commercial, including the new bar in the Ritz, London.

• Influenced by Renzo Mongiardino and Geoffrey Bennison • The Prince Regent and Napoleon are icons on account of their lavish design styles • Would ban congestion charging and introduce the death penalty for dogs which foul pavements • Addicted to feather beds and playing cards.

mk decoration

Designer: Merve Kurttepeli Gürsel. Company: MK Decoration, Istanbul, Turkey. Projects: Large period townhouses on the Bosphorus in Istanbul.

• Dreams of living in a yali (early nineteenth century Ottoman house) by the water • Reads history books, wears Galliano, stays Blakes Hotel • Addicted to her family, Sundays at home are the true luxury.

'I love conjuring up the concept of a united world'

louise bradley

Designer: Louise Bradley. Company: Louise Bradley, London, UK. Projects: Exclusive residential in central London.

'Good design is all about detail. I can easily admit that such a mantra has allowed design to totally take over my life'

• Dreams of living in the middle of nowhere bu
not without her dachshund • Stays Prince Mauric
Hotel in Mauritius • Watches Chocolat, listen
Emma Shaplin, worships Tom Ford • Hates swamps

'Too neutral a scheme can appear bland and lifeless'

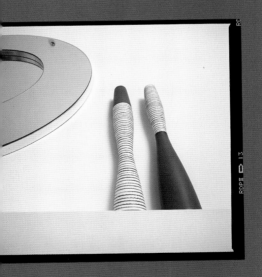

Designer: Christopher Dezille.
Company: Honky Design, London,
UK. Projects: High-end urban
apartments in new developments,
including many show flats.

• Turns on his espresso machine the first minute he wakes • Would instigate a four day week and ban smoking • Listens to Radiohead, rides Harley Davidson, wears Fake London • Icons: Eames, Jacobsen, Gaudi.

'I like to give a minimal scheme a fun lift with directional, specially commissioned artwork or brightly coloured textiles'

'I am offering clients a
lifestyle, rather than a look'

interiøret

Designer: Hanne Hovland. Company: Interiøret, Oslo, Norway. Projects: Second homes in the Norwegian mountains.

• Already has the homes of her dreams: a mountain cabin and a cottage by the sea • Respects all creatives from Jamie Oliver to the ancient Egyptians • Likes piano concertos, spa treatments, dinner with her husband

'I'm not into classicism. My style is simple but rich, traditional and modern'

joseph sy associates

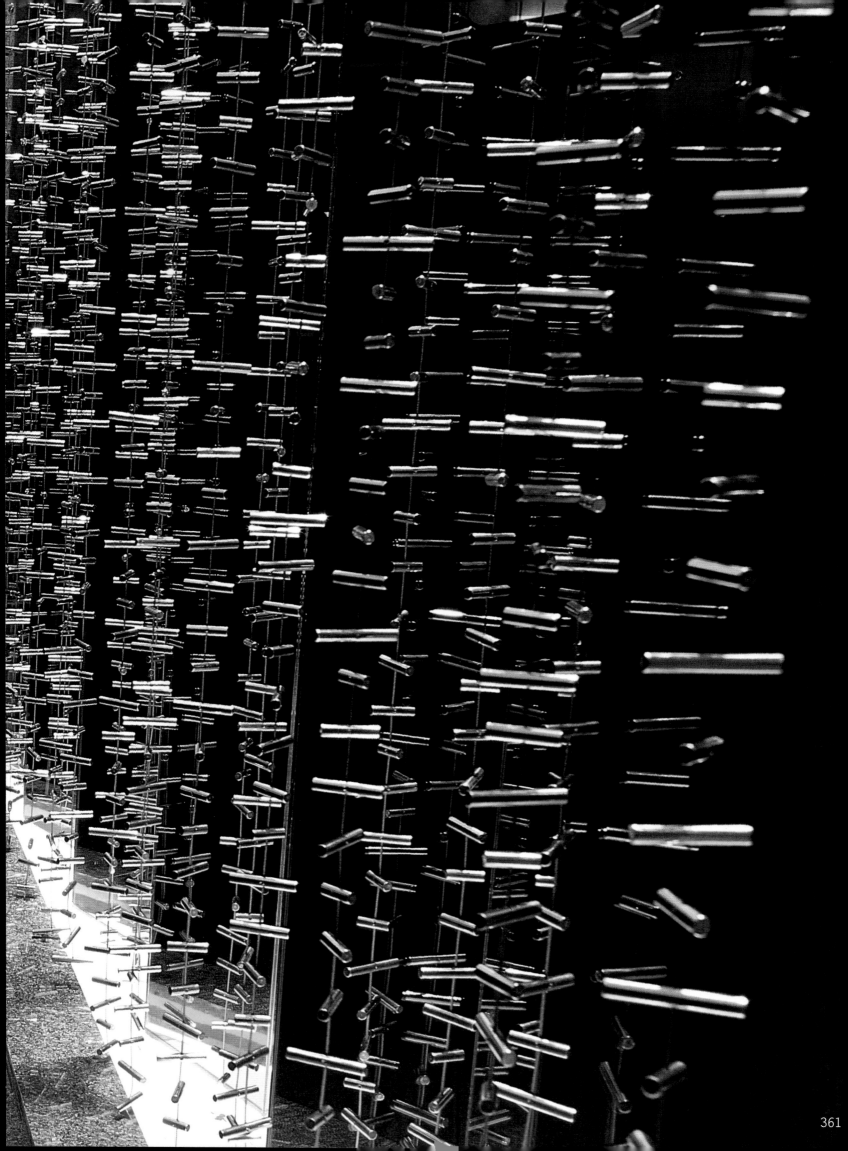

Designer: Joseph Sy. Company: Joseph Sy Associates, Hong Kong. Projects: Restaurants, shops and residential in Hong Kong and China.

• Would ban excess and over design in small spaces • Empty space is the great luxury • Likes the work of Tom Ford for its simplicity and Norman Foster's for its complexity • Driven by work, addicted to art, proudest of his daughter,

'Its very important to create a centre piece, a punch line

'Lighting is my most essential material'

directory of designers

4 Zeynep Fadillioglu
ZF Design, Ahmet Adnan Saygun Cad,
Dag Apt no. 72/5, Ulus,
Istanbul, Turkey
t: 0090 21 22 87 09 36
f: 0090 21 22 87 09 94
e: www.design@zfdesign.com
www.zfdesign.com

12 Rabih Hage
69-71 Sloane Avenue,
London SW3 3DH
t: 0207 823 8288
f: 0207 823 8258
e: info@rabih-hage.com
www.rabih-hage.com

20 B.V.B.A. Giardini
Kapellensteenweg 544,
2920 Heide Kalmthout, Belgium
t: 0032 366 67 417
f: 0032 366 60 056

28 Kit Kemp
Firmdale Hotels,
18 Thurloe Place,
London SW7 2SP
t: 0207 581 4045
f: 0207 581 1867
e: KitKemp@Firmdale.com

38 John Solomon Design
48 Ham Street,
Richmond, Surrey TW10 7HT
t: 0208 940 2444
f: 0208 940 1188
e: mail@jsajsd.com
www.jsajsd.com

44 Taylor Howes Designs
208 The Chambers, Chelsea Harbour
London SW10 0XF
t: 0207 349 9017
f: 0207 349 9018

54 Jane Ainscough Design
Ohnsorweg 11, Hamburg 22605,
Germany
f: 0049 40 8664469
e: info@janeainscough.com

62 Hennie Interiors
Bennechesgt 1, 0169 Oslo,
Norway
t: 0047 22 06 85 86
f: 0047 22 06 85 87

70 Cream
12F Capital Comm. Building,
26 Leighton Road, Causeway Bay,
Hong Kong
t: 00852 2147 1297
f: 00852 2147 0118
e: info@cream.com.hk
www.cream.com.hk

78 Joao Mansur
R. Groenlandia, 1922b-Jd. America,
Sao Paulo, Brazil CEP 01434-100
t: 0055 11 3083 15 00
f: 0055 11 3081 77 32
e: joaomansur@uol.com.br

88 Tara Bernerd
Target Living
6 Pont Street,
London SW1X 9EL
t: 0207 823 2316
f: 0207 823 2317
e: target@targetliving.com

96 Wixon Gibbs
The Studio, 17 Broad Lane,
Hampton, Middlesex TW12 3AL
t: 0208 979 4608
f: 0208 941 7717
www.wixongibbs.co.uk

104 Isherwood Interior Design
12 Imperial Square,
Cheltenham,
Gloucestershire GL50 1QB
t: 01242 226 966
f: 01242 227 444
www.isherwoodinteriordesign.com

110 Christopher Chang
Interior Design
53 route de Chene, CH-1208,
Geneva, Switzerland
t: 0041 22 70 05 831
f: 0041 22 70 05 832
e: ccid@bluewin.ch

118 Claudia Pelizzari
Interior Design
Piazza Tebaldo Brusato 5,
25121 Brescia, Italy
t: 0039 030 377 1320
f: 0039 030 377 0172
e: info@pelizzari.com
www.pelizzari.com

126 Monica Blinco Interior Design
Unit 30/70 Vernon Terrace,
Teneriffe, Brisbane, Queensland,
Australia
t: 0061 73216 1665
f: 0061 73216 1848
e: blinco@ozemail.com.au

132 Lifestyles Interiors
48 Old Church Street,
London SW3 5BY
t: 0207 349 8020
f: 0207 349 8021
e: jo@northacre.co.uk

142 Andrew Winch Designs
The Old Fire Station,
123 Mortlake High Street,
London SW14 8SN
t: 0208 392 8400
f: 0208 392 8401
e: info@andrew-winch-designs.co.uk

150 Merrion Square Interiors
The Design Company,
82 Merrion Square,
Dublin 2, Ireland
t: 0035 31 676 5040
f: 0035 31 662 8473

158 Broosk Saib
4 Heathrise, Kersfield Road,
London SW15 3HF
t/f: 0208 788 5130

168 Serdar Gülgün
Husrev Gerede, Caddesi Gozum,
Apt. no. 69 D.3 80200 Tesvikiye,
Istanbul, Turkey
t: 0090 212 261 1840
f: 0090 212 261 6084
e: serdargulgun@hotmail.com

174 Jacobs Design
169 Stewart Drive, Tiburon,
California 94920, U.S.A.
t: 001 415 435 0520
f: 001 415 435 3604
e: jerry@jerryjacobsdesign.com
www.jerryjacobsdesign.com

182 Casa Nova
Konigsallee 30,
D 40212 Dusseldorf, Germany
t: 0049 211 326 952
f: 0049 211 328 446

190 Vie Interieur Architecture et
D'ecoration D'interieur
Rue de l'hopital 24,
2000 Neuchatel, Suisse
t: 0041 32 721 1800
f: 0041 32 721 1800
e: vie_interieur@bluewin.ch
www.vieinterieur.ch

194 Irma McPherson Interior Design
14 Durban Road, Wynberg,
Cape Town 7800, South Africa
t/f: 0207 21797 0125
e: mcpherson@iafrica.com

200 Marc Hertrich Interior Design
15 rue Gambey, 75011 Paris, France
t: 00331 43 14 00 00
f: 00331 43 14 00 22
e: contact@marchertrich.com
www.marchertrich.com

206 Chhada, Siembieda
& Associates
Suite 2105, 21st Floor,
118 Connaught Road West,
Hong Kong
t: 00852 2521 2191 / 2521 4111
f: 00852 2810 6061
e: csal@chhadasiembieda.com.hk

212 Azul-Tierra
Angel Lozano 2,
03001 Alicante, Spain
t: 0034 965 20 83 40
f: 0034 965 14 02 03

220 Interiors Bis
60 Sloane Avenue,
London SW3 3DD
t: 0207 838 1104
f: 0207 838 1105
e: info@interiorsbis.com
www.interiorsbis.com

226 Manuel Francisco Jorge
Interiores
Rua das Flores,
105-2. Esq. 1200-194 Lisbon,
Portugal
t: 00351 213 424 294
f: 00351 213 424 295
e: mfj@netcabo.pt

230 Sue Rohrer
Chapfstrasse 106,
CH-8126, Zumikon, Switzerland
t: 0041 1919 0290
f: 0041 1919 0288

238 Artus Inneneinrichtung
Grabenstrasse 11,
CH-6300 Zug, Switzerland
t: 0041 41 712 2840
f: 0041 41 712 2841
e: artus-ag@bluewin.ch
www.artus-ag.ch

244 Jestico and Whiles
1 Coburg Street,
London NW1 2HP
t: 0207 380 0382
f: 0207 380 0511

252 Sriberg Associates
13a Nevern Mansions,
42 Warwick Road,
London SW5 9TJ
t: 0207 370 6959
f: 0207 370 6959

258 Michael Attenborough
Radisson Edwardian Hotels
140 Bath Road, Hayes,
Middlesex, UB3 5AW
t: 0208 817 2528
f: 0208 757 7949

264 Associates III
1516 Blake Street,
Denver, Co 80202,
U.S.A.
t: 001 303 534 4444
f: 001 303 629 5035

272 Artistic Design
103001 U1 Spiridonovka,
9/2 KV. 070, Russia
t: 007 095 203 3397
f: 007 095 258 5202

280 DQ&W Design
PO Box 51577, Waterfront,
Cape Town 8002,
South Africa
m: 0027 82 896 5803
m: 0027 82 857 8252
f: 0027 21 433 0240
e: dqwdesign@freemail.absa.co.za

286 Hunt Hamilton Zuch
The Studio, 26 Ives Street,
London SW3 2ND
t: 0207 581 6601
f: 0207 581 6602
e: HHZ@easynet.co.uk
e: Lynne.HHZ@btconnect.com

290 Constanze Interior Projects
81 Mount Ararat Road,
Richmond,
Surrey TW10 6PL
t: 0208 948 5533
f: 0208 940 9797
e: constanze@constanze.co.uk
www.constanze.co.uk

296 B. Pila Design Studio
5001 SW 74 Ct.
Suite 104, Miami, Fl 33155,
U.S.A.
t: 001 305 668 6616
f: 001 305 668 6617
e: info@bpiladesign.com
www.bpiladesign.com

302 Sabi Sabi
Private Game Reserve
85 Central Street,
Houghton Estate,
Johannesburg,
South Africa
t: 0027 11 483 3939
f: 0027 11 483 3799
e: com@sabisabi.com
www.sabisabi.com

308 Kelly Hoppen Interiors
2 Munden Street,
London W14 0RH
t: 0207 471 3350
f: 0207 471 3351

314 S.B. Interiors
Hotel Marbella Club,
Galeria Comercial Local 5,
Marbella 29600,
Spain
t: 0034 952 86 45 45
f: 0034 952 77 04 70

322 Thorp Design
10 Peterborough Mews,
London SW6 3BL
t: 0207 731 6887
f: 0207 731 0095
e: office@thorp.co.uk

328 Tessa Kennedy Design
Studio 5, 2 Olaf Steet,
London W11 4BE
t: 0207 221 4546
f: 0207 229 2899
e: info@tessakennedydesign.com
www.tessakennedydesign.com

332 MK Decoration
ABDI, Ipekci Caddesi,
Lalezar Apt. no. 45/5,
Tesvikiye 80200,
Istanbul,
Turkey
t: 0090 212 296 5671
f: 0090 212 233 2372
e: mervegursel@turk.net

338 Louise Bradley
15 Walton Street,
London SW3 2HX
t: 0207 589 1442
f: 0207 589 2009

344 Christopher Dezille
Honky Design
19 Loubet Street,
London SW17 9HD
t: 07786 131186
f: 0208 672 1765

352 Interioret Hanne Hovland
Nobelsgate 23, 0368,
Oslo,
Norway
t: 0047 22 55 07 04
f: 0047 22 55 18 14
e: hanne.hovland@interioret.no

360 Joseph Sy Associates
17/F Heng Shan Centre,
145 Queen's Road East,
Hong Kong
t: 0085 22 86 61 333
f: 0085 22 86 61 222